SPOOKY RIDDLES and JOKES

by JOSEPH ROSENBLOOM

PICTURES by Sanford HOFFMAN

Sterling Publishing Co., Inc. New York

To Mr. David Boehm

Library of Congress Cataloging-in-Publication Data

Rosenbloom, Joseph.
  Spooky riddles and jokes.

  Includes Index.
  Summary: A collection of over 700 riddles and jokes
about things that go bump in the night, in such categories
as "This Will Slay You!" and "Wild and Weird."
  1. Supernatural—Juvenile humor. 2. Wit and humor,
Juvenile. 3. Riddles, Juvenile. [1. Riddles.
2. Jokes] I. Hoffman, Sanford, ill. II. Title.
PN6231.S877R67 1987   818'.5402   87-17972
ISBN 0-8069-6576-2
ISBN 0-8069-6577-0 (lib. bdg.)

5   7   9   10   8   6   4

Copyright © 1987 by Joseph Rosenbloom
Published by Sterling Publishing Co., Inc.
Two Park Avenue, New York, N.Y. 10016
Distributed in Canada by Oak Tree Press Ltd.
℅ Canadian Manda Group, P.O. Box 920, Station U
Toronto, Ontario, Canada M8Z 5P9
Distributed in Great Britain and Europe by Cassell PLC
Artillery House, Artillery Row, London SW1P 1RT, England
Distributed in Australia by Capricorn Ltd.
P.O. Box 665, Lane Cove, NSW 2066
Manufactured in the United States of America

Contents

Books by Joseph Rosenbloom

Biggest Riddle Book in the World
Daffy Definitions
Doctor Knock-Knock's Official Knock-Knock
  Dictionary
Funniest Dinosaur Book Ever!
Funniest Joke Book Ever!
Funniest Knock-Knock Book Ever!
Funniest Riddle Book Ever!
Funny Insults & Snappy Put-Downs
Gigantic Joke Book
Giggles, Gags· & Groaners
Knock-Knock! Who's There?
Looniest Limerick Book in the World
Mad Scientist
Monster Madness
Nutty Knock Knocks!
Official Wild West Joke Book
Ridiculous Nicholas Haunted House Riddles
Ridiculous Nicholas Pet Riddles
Ridiculous Nicholas Riddle Book
Silly Verse (and Even Worse)
696 Silly School Jokes & Riddles
Wacky Insults and Terrible Jokes
Zaniest Riddle Book in the World

1. SWIFTIES

What do little ghosts wear when it rains?
BOO-ts.

What do little ghouls wear in the rain?
Ghoul-oshes (galoshes).

What is a little ghost's favorite type of music?
Haunting melodies.

What is a little ghost's favorite amusement park ride?
The roller ghost-er.

What makes the letter "G" so scary?
It turns your host into a ghost.

What is spookier than a ghost?
Two ghosts.

On what day do ghosts make the most noise?
  Moan-day.

What is the best place to see a ghost?
  About a mile away.

What do ghosts put on their hair?
  Scare (hair) spray.

How do ghosts like to fly?
  Ghost-to-ghost (coast-to-coast).

What do you call a vampire that flies first class in a 747?
  A passenger.

What is big and hairy and flies 1,200 miles per hour?
King Kongcorde.

What has a broom and flies?
A janitor with an airline ticket.

What has fur and flies?
A dead werewolf.

How do you keep a werewolf from smelling?
Cut off its nose.

How do you keep a werewolf from chewing up the back seat of a car?
Make him sit up front.

What does a werewolf do when traffic is snarled?
It snarls back.

What would you get if you crossed a werewolf and a rooster?
An animal that howls when the sun comes up.

What would you get if you crossed a chicken and a ghost?
A poultry-geist (poltergeist).

Which monster comes from New England?
A Vermonster.

What is green and comes out at night?
Vampickle.

What looks like a pickle, has a lot of teeth and lives in a swamp?
A crocodill.

How do zombies send messages through a swamp?
By moss code.

How do sharks send messages through the ocean?
By Morse cod.

Why did the shark cross the ocean?
To get to the other tide.

How do deaf sharks hear?
With a herring aid.

What would you get if you crossed a rooster and a shark?
Chicken of the Sea.

What would you get if a rooster was fresh with King Kong?
Creamed chicken.

What is dead, ugly and has a red nose?
Rudolf the Red-Nosed Zombie.

What is a zombie's favorite rock?
Tombstone.

What is a little zombie's favorite stuffed animal?
Its deady bear.

What is the hardest thing to sell a zombie?
Life insurance.

How can you shoot a monster without making him mad at you?
Use your camera.

How do you shoot a killer bee?
With a BB gun.

How do you keep a dragon from going through the eye of a needle?

Tie a knot in its tail.

Where do you find the most famous dragons?
In the Hall of Flame.

Where do you get dragon milk?
From short cows.

When does a monster wring its hands?
When the bell is out of order.

Where does a monster keep its hands?
In a hand bag.

SHOVING GIANTS AROUND

How do you get a giant into a frying pan?
Use shortening.

How do you get a giant into a pencil box?
Take the pencils out first.

How do you get a giant out of the cornflakes?
Follow the instructions on the box.

How do you get six giants out of a small car?
The same way they got in.

What goes "Ha-ha-ha—plop!"?
A monster laughing its head off.

What goes "Thud, thud, thud, squish"?
A monster with a wet sneaker.

What is big and ugly and goes, "Slam, slam, slam, slam"?
A four-door monster.

What is three stories tall, green and tastes sweet?
The Jelly Green Giant.

What resembles a blob but has chrome stripes?
A deluxe blob.

How can you tell if there is a giant in your lunch box?
The lid won't close.

Why couldn't Godzilla hide behind the mountain?
Because the mountain peaks (peeks).

LOU: Would you rather have King Kong attack you—or Godzilla?
SUE: I'd rather have them attack each other.

What did Godzilla say
when he met King Kong?
  "Small world, isn't it?"

How do demons stage a protest?
They demon-strate.

What is the best way to get rid of demons?
Exorcise (exercise).

What happens if you don't pay your exorcist?
You get repossessed.

What is gray, has big teeth and prevents forest fires?

Smokey the Shark.

Who lives in a casket, wears a cape and doesn't want to be seen?

A vampire who is playing hookey from school.

Where does a vampire keep its cash?

In the blood bank.

What did Count Dracula say when he called the blood bank?

"Do you deliver?"

What does a vampire get when it bites a mummy?

Practice.

What would you get if you crossed a monster and a goose?

A creature that honks before it runs you over.

What would you get if you crossed a monster and a rabbit?

I don't know what you'd call it, but you'd have hundreds in a couple of weeks.

What would you get if you crossed a snail and Count Dracula?

The world's slowest vampire.

How does a vampire file its teeth?

Under the letter "T."

How do you say vampire in Spanish?
 "Vampire in Spanish."

"Doctor, doctor! I keep thinking I'm invisible!"
 "Who said that?"

TIP: What's so unusual about the Invisible Man?
TOP: You don't see one every day.

What would you get if you crossed a witch and an insect?
 A spelling bee.

How do witches tell time?
 With a witch watch.

How do you make a witch scratch?
 Take away its "W".

Where does the Abominable Snowman keep its money?
 In a snowbank.

What money does the Abominable Snowman keep?
 Cold cash.

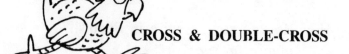

CROSS & DOUBLE-CROSS

Why did the evil chicken cross the road?
For foul (fowl) purposes.

Why did the evil chicken cross the road and then cross back again?
Because he was a double crosser.

Why did the Frankenstein monster cross the road?
It was the chicken's day off.

Why didn't the zombie cross the road?
It didn't want to be mistaken for a chicken.

Why did the one-armed gremlin cross the road?
To get to the secondhand store.

Why didn't the skeleton cross the road?
Because it had no guts.

What was Godzilla doing in the middle of the road?
Catching the chickens that tried to get to the other side.

Why did King Kong scratch his nose?
Because that's where he itched.

When does King Kong roar?
Any time he wants to.

What is the best way to listen to King Kong's roar?
On an ape recorder.

How can you tell a skeleton from King Kong?
It's hard to get into a revolving door with King Kong.

What would you get if you crossed King Kong and a parrot?

I don't know, but you better give it a cracker when it asks for one.

What would you get if you crossed a parrot and a crocodile?

An animal that talks your head off.

What would you get if you crossed a cocker spaniel, a poodle and a ghost?

A cock-a-poodle-boo!

2. HAZARDOUS TO YOUR HEALTH

What is white, cold and lives in a nuclear reactor?

The Atom-inable Snowman.

What would you get if you crossed the Abominable Snowman and an eye doctor?

Good ice sight (eyesight).

What would you get if you crossed the Abominable Snowman and a terrific employment agency?

A big snow job.

What is the Abominable Snowman's favorite song?

"There's no business like snow business . . ."

What has sixteen wheels and breathes fire?
A dragon on roller skates.

Why is a dragon big, green and scaly?
If it was little, white and smooth, it would be a Tic-Tac.

What branch of the service did the little phantom want to join when it grew up?
The Ghost Guard.

What branch of the service did the little werewolf want to join?
The Hair Corps.

What goes, "Flap, flap, flap, swoosh! Flap, flap, flap, swoosh!"?

Count Dracula caught in a revolving door.

What is better than presence of mind when you meet Count Dracula on a dark night?

Absence of body.

VAMPIRE: I want to drink your blood!

VICTIM: Sorry, I already gave at the office.

SPOOKY BESTSELLERS

1. *Screams in the Dark* by I. C. Fingers
2. *The Haunted House* by Terry Fide
3. *The Invisible Man* by Donna C. Hugh
4. *The Open Coffin* by Bea Ware
5. *The Evil Monster* by Upton O. Goode
6. *The Mummy's Tomb* by Don Gogh Wynne
7. *Land of the Mummies* by E.Gypt Shun
8. *A Mummy Confesses* by I. M. Dedd
9. *Mystery of the Bones* by S. Kelly Tonne
10. *Is This House Haunted?* by Howard I. Noh

What is wrapped in bandages and goes, "Click, click, click?"

A ballpoint mummy.

What is covered in bandages and has a bright red bow?

A gift-wrapped mummy.

What has bandages and flies?

A mummy covered with jelly.

What would you get if you crossed a mummy and a skunk?

A dirty look from the mummy.

What would you get if you crossed a giant and a skunk?

A big stink.

What would you get if you crossed the Frankenstein monster and a skunk?

Don't do it! The Frankenstein monster doesn't like to be crossed.

What would you get if you crossed a shark with a zebra?

A toothy killer in a striped suit.

Why wasn't the girl afraid of the shark?
It was a man-eating shark.

JO: I saw a man-eating shark in the aquarium.
MO: That's nothing. I saw a man eating shrimp in the cafeteria.

THAT MONSTER IS SO MEAN

HOW MEAN IS HE?

He's so mean, he won't eat anything that agrees with him.

He's so mean, even an echo won't answer him back.

He's so mean, even fleas won't get close to him.

What comes out at night and goes, "Flap, flap, flap, OUCH!"?
A vampire with a sore tooth.

What is the difference between a vampire with a sore tooth and a stormy day?
One roars with pain; the other pours with rain.

Why did the vampire go to the dentist?
To improve his bite.

What time was it when Count Dracula went to the dentist?
Tooth-hurty (2:30).

Why does Count Dracula brush his teeth after every meal?
To prevent bat-breath.

What does a polite vampire say after he bites his victim?
"It's been nice gnawing you."

How do you stop the pain of vampire bites?
Don't bite any.

How do you treat a sick monster?
With respect.

Where do witches go when they get sick?
To the witch doctor.

Why do witches fly broomsticks?
They don't have tricycles.

What does a witch do when her broom is broken?
She witch hikes.

How does a werewolf with fleas get around?
He itch hikes.

What would you get if you crossed a jolly fat man in a red suit with a werewolf?

Santa Claws.

Who went into the werewolf's den and came out alive?

The werewolf.

What would you say if you were in the woods and came face to face with a werewolf?

"Help!"

How do you stop a monster from charging?

Take away his credit cards.

What should you do if a monster charges you?

Pay him.

SPOOKY HOW-TO BOOKS

1. *Building Monsters* by A. Cy. N. Tyst
2. *Body Snatching* by Robin Graves
3. *How to Quiet a Werewolf* by Justin Casey Howells
4. *Treating Werewolves* by Yvette N. Arian
5. *Gravedigging* by U. Greta Shovel
6. *Arguing with Monsters* by Yul B. Sorry
7. *Monster Making as a Hobby* by Dr. Frank N. Stine
8. *What to Say to a Zombie* by Hugo Way
9. *Living With Vampires* by Minerva S. Wreck
10. *Ghost Hunter in the Arctic* by R. U. Cole and I. M. Freezon

What would you get if you crossed a train going 80 miles an hour and an auto going 55 miles an hour?

A big funeral.

What would you get if you crossed a rattlesnake and a funeral?

A hiss and a hearse.

What is the first thing a ghost does when it gets into a car?

It boo-ckles up its sheet belt.

FIRST MONSTER: Quick—call me a taxi!

SECOND MONSTER: Okay—you're a taxi. But to tell the truth, you look more like a two-ton pick-up truck.

Count Dracula was lying in his coffin when some boys nailed roller skates to it and pushed it down a hill. It narrowly missed cars and people and finally crashed into a drugstore. As it rolled by, Count Dracula lifted the lid, stuck his head out and said to the pharmacist, "Do you have anything to stop this coffin?"

NURSE: Doctor, the Invisible Man is outside.
DOCTOR: Tell him I can't see him.

What monster has red spots?
The one with measles.

What do you do when King Kong breaks his big toe?
Call a big toe (tow) truck.

How do you fix King Kong?
With a monkey wrench.

Did you hear about the monster who liked to stop where they served truck drivers?

What did the monster eat after the dentist pulled its tooth?
The dentist.

LEM: Did you hear about the monster rip-off?
CLEM: No, what was the rip-off?
LEM: Oh, arms, legs, heads . . .

What do you do when Godzilla sneezes?
  Get out of the way.

What would you get if Godzilla stepped on Batman and Robin?
  Flatman and Ribbon.

What would you get if you crossed Godzilla and a chicken?
  The biggest cluck you ever saw.

What would you get if you crossed Godzilla and a mole?
  The Panama Canal.

WILLY MONSTER: You know the Panama Canal? Well, my father dug it.
TILLY MONSTER: You know the Dead Sea? Well, my father killed it.

What disease do vampires fear most?
  Tooth decay.

What disease do vampires hate most?
  A stiff neck.

Why do black widow spiders spin webs?
  Because they don't know how to knit.

A PAGE FROM THE ANNALS OF CRIME

What was Jack the Ripper's middle name?
The.

What skeleton was a famous detective?
Sherlock Bones.

Why don't the police ever arrest skeletons?
Because it's hard to pin anything on them.

Why was the dragon arrested for speeding?
He burned up the road.

Why did the ghoul leave a pail in the middle of the road?
He hoped someone would kick the bucket.

Who lived in the ocean, had eight legs and was a killer?
Billy the Squid.

How do you run over a dragon?
Jump on its head, run along its back and slide down its tail.

What hope is there when you see a werewolf?
The hope that he hasn't seen you.

What would you get if you crossed a werewolf and a vampire?
A fur coat that sticks to your neck.

How do you get fur from a werewolf?
By car, bus, train or plane.

"Doctor, you've got to help me! I feel like a werewolf!"
"Sit!"

What did the man say when he saw four werewolves, wearing sunglasses, coming over a hill?
Nothing. He didn't recognize them.

3. THIS WILL SLAY YOU!

ANNOUNCER (*on TV horror show*): "The Invisible Man" will not be seen tonight.

What is King Tut's favorite TV show?
"Name That Tomb."

Which game show do sharks watch?
"Name That Tuna."

What is the soft, mushy stuff between a shark's teeth?
Slow swimmers.

What old-time comedian lived in the ocean and ate slow swimmers?
Groucho Sharks (Marx).

What would you get if you crossed a comedian and a hangman?
A practical choker.

The executioner was taking the prisoner to his place of execution a mile away. It was a rainy, stormy day.

"What a terrible day to die," sighed the condemned man.

"What are you complaining about?" said the executioner. "I have to walk all the way back in the rain."

THE LETTER "S" IS SO DANGEROUS—

HOW DANGEROUS IS IT?

It's so dangerous it makes cream scream.

It's so dangerous it turns lime into slime.

It's so dangerous it changes laughter to slaughter.

What did the condemned man say when they saved him from hanging?

"No noose is good noose!"

What candy did the condemned man want after his last meal?

Life Savers.

What happened to the bad egg?

It was eggs-ecuted.

What happened to the bad picture?

It got hung.

What would you get if you crossed a mummy and Jesse James?

A band-aid bandit.

What would you get if you crossed Jesse James and Count Dracula?

A hold-up at the blood bank.

What happened to Jesse James after he met Count Dracula?

He was a sick shooter.

CUSTOMER (*at carnival*): That knife-throwing act was terrible. I want my money back.

CARNIVAL OWNER: What was the matter with it?

CUSTOMER: Call that a knife-thrower? He got ten chances and didn't even hit that girl once!

The agent called the actor. "I've got some good news and some bad news."

"Quick," said the actor, "what's the good news?"

"The good news is that you will star in a new film."

"Wow—fame at last! My face will be recognized everywhere! But what's the bad news?"

"You will be playing the Invisible Man."

Did you hear about the vampire who went to Hollywood? All he could get were bit parts.

SAM: I'm going to watch *The Green Monster from the Red Swamp* on television tonight.

PAM: Don't you mean *The Red Monster from the Green Swamp?*

SAM: It makes no difference to me. I have a black-and-white set.

NAN: How did you like that new vampire movie?
DAN: It was Fang-tastic!

What's a geologist's favorite scary movie?
  "The Rocky Horror Show."

What do you say about a bad mummy movie?
  "It Sphinx!"

What is a ghoul's favorite musical show?
  "My Fear Lady."

What is a zombie's favorite Shakespeare play?
  "Romeo & Ghouliet."

JOKES YOU WON'T
GET TO HEAR

Did you hear the joke about the grave?
Never mind. You wouldn't dig it.

Did you hear the joke about the quicksand?
Never mind. It takes too long to sink in.

Did you hear the joke about the executioner?
Never mind. You wouldn't get the hang of it.

Did you hear the joke about the Abominable Snowman?
Never mind. It would only leave you cold.

Did you hear the joke about the mummy?
Never mind. It's old stuff.

Did you hear the joke about the giant?
Never mind. It's over your head.

JOKES YOU WON'T GET TO HEAR

Did you hear the joke about the fire-breathing dragon?

Never mind. It would burn you up.

Did you hear the joke about the vampire's teeth?

Never mind. You wouldn't get the point.

Did you hear the joke about the monster that never took a bath?

Never mind. It's a dirty story.

Did you hear the joke about the 2,000-year-old bread?

Never mind. It's kind of stale.

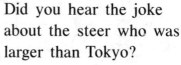

Did you hear the joke about the steer who was larger than Tokyo?

Never mind. It's a lot of bull.

Why is it so hard to play a joke on a snake?
You can't pull its leg.

Did Dr. Frankenstein make his monster laugh?
Yes, he kept him in stitches.

What is the best way to get big laughs?
Tell jokes to the Jolly Green Giant.

When do zombies laugh?
When they make ghouls of themselves.

When do skeletons laugh?
When you tickle their funny bone.

Dr. Frankenstein sent Igor, his assistant, to fetch two fresh bodies. Igor found a grave marked, "John and Emily Hill." While Dr. Frankenstein worked on the bodies, he asked Igor to turn on the stereo. As soon as the music started, the two bodies sprang up from the table.

"How wonderful," said Dr. Frankenstein. "The Hills are alive with the sound of music."

Who is Count Dracula's favorite singer?
Fang Sinatra.

Who is Dracula's favorite composer?
Ludwig van Bat-hoven (Beethoven).

What did Ludwig van Beethoven do after he died?
He decomposed.

What musical note do you hear when Godzilla walks through a ranch?
Beef-flat.

What musical note do you hear when Godzilla steps on a coal mine?
A-flat miner (minor).

Where can you find popular ghost songs?
In sheet music.

What musical instrument do skeletons play?
The trom-BONE.

Why don't skeletons ever play church music?
They don't have organs.

What song does Dracula sing in December?
"I'm screaming of a bite Christmas . . ."

What song is popular among monsters at Christmas?
"Deck the halls with poison ivy, fa-la-la . . ."

What do you call a group of zombie dancers?
A corpse (corps) de ballet.

RAY: There I was—the Frankenstein monster was on one side, a mummy on the other, and a werewolf was getting ready to pounce. I let out an awful shriek.
MAY: What happened?
RAY: The usher told me if it happened again, I'd have to leave the theatre.

4. FAMILY TIES

Why is the Dracula family so close?
Because blood is thicker than water.

What do you call monster parents?
Mummies and deadies.

What do you call the mother and father of invisible children?
Transparents.

What do you call a monster who eats his father and mother?
An orphan.

MONSTER WIFE (*to* MONSTER HUSBAND): Don't just stand there—slay something!

Why did the giant's mother knit him three socks for his birthday?
Because he grew another foot.

THAT MONSTER BABY IS SO UGLY—

*HOW UGLY
IS HE?*

He's so ugly, his parents sent him back and kept the stork.

He's so ugly, when he was born the doctor slapped his mother.

He's so ugly, his face is like a flower—a cauliflower.

He's so ugly, his face is like a banana without its skin—no appeal.

What does a witch's broom say to its child?
   "Go to sweep, little baby."

The father monster was explaining to a neighbor that he had found a quick way to get his baby to sleep.

"I toss him up in the air again and again," he said.

"How does that put your baby to sleep?" asked the neighbor.

"We have low ceilings."

MONSTER (*to another* MONSTER): When your grandfather was born, they passed out candy. When your father was born, they passed out flowers. When you were born, they just passed out.

FATHER MONSTER: Why does our little boy have so many holes in his forehead?

MOTHER MONSTER: Isn't that cute? He's learning to eat with a fork.

What state do ghosts live in?
They don't live in a state. They live in a terror-tory (territory).

Where in town do zombies live?
On a dead end street.

FIRST GIANT: Are you going to take the five o'clock train home?

SECOND GIANT: No, I don't think I can get it through the door.

What happened when the house was taken over by ghosts?

The fire went out, the steam escaped, the rope skipped, the eggs scrambled, the milk evaporated, the scissors cut out and the stockings ran.

DON: The Frankenstein monster helped beautify our neighborhood.

RON: How did he do that?

DON: He moved away.

When is a vampire not a vampire?
When it turns into a haunted house.

What has 400 teeth and says "Haunted House"?
A picket fence with a sign on it.

How do you open a haunted house?
With a skeleton key.

What is spookier than the outside of a haunted house?

The inside.

Which part of a house do ghouls like best?

The die-ning (dining) room.

Why is the kitchen the most violent room in the house?

Because that's where you beat the eggs, whip the cream and batter the fish.

Where do ghouls hang up their coats?

In the croak room.

What room makes a mummy nervous?
The living room.

What do mummies talk about when they get together?
Old times.

Why did the mummy sit on the stove?
She wanted to be the last of the red hot mummies.

LITTLE SNAKE: I hope I'm not poisonous.
MOTHER SNAKE: Why, dear?
LITTLE SNAKE: I just bit my tongue.

Why did the baby snake cry?
It lost its rattle.

Why are so many zombies sitting around all day?
They don't need to work for a living.

DORIS GHOUL: Please don't sit in that chair.
MORRIS GHOUL: Why not?
DORIS GHOUL: We're saving it for Rigor Mortis to set in.

Why did the monsters keep their son in the refrigerator?
So he wouldn't get spoiled.

How can you tell if King Kong has been in your refrigerator?
By the tracks in the butter.

How can you tell if King Kong is visiting your house?
His skateboard will be parked outside.

What time is it when King Kong knocks on your door?
Time to get a new door.

AUNT MONSTER: Why did you wrap barbed wire around the banister?
FATHER MONSTER: Because Junior slides down the banister all the time.
AUNT MONSTER: The barbed wire stops him?
FATHER MONSTER: No—but it slows him down.

LITTLE MONSTER: But, Mom, don't you think Uncle Max deserves a decent burial?

FATHER MONSTER: Shut up, kid, and keep flushing.

LITTLE MONSTER: Mom—the garbage man is here!

MOTHER MONSTER: Tell him to leave three cans.

MONSTER BOY: Mommy, mommy! The lawn mower cut off my leg!

MOTHER MONSTER: Well, stay outside until it stops bleeding. I just mopped the floor.

MONSTER GIRL: Mommy, it's getting hot in here. Can I open the door?

MOTHER MONSTER: Certainly not! Do you want the fire to spread to the rest of the house?

"Suzy!" said the mother ghoul, "for the last time, either you stop playing with your brother—or I shut the coffin!"

What happened when the werewolf fell into the washing machine?

He became a wash-and-werewolf.

Where do sea monsters wash?

In the river basin.

What did one sea monster say to the other sea monster?

"Am I my brother's kipper?"

What did King Kong say when his sister had a baby?

"Well, I'll be a monkey's uncle!"

What did the Invisible Man always say to his children?

"You should be heard and not seen."

What did the mummy say when her child misbehaved?

"Tut, tut."

FIRST MONSTER: Would you join me in a cup of tea?

SECOND MONSTER: Certainly—you get in first.

BABY MONSTER: Is it all right to eat pickles with your fingers?

MOTHER MONSTER: No, eat the pickles first. *Then* eat your fingers.

MOTHER MONSTER: Junior, what on earth are you doing?

LITTLE MONSTER: I'm chasing a man around a tree.

MOTHER MONSTER: How many times must I tell you not to play with your food!

DON'T SAY IT!

What can't you say to the Invisible Man?
"Disappear!"

What can't you say to a zombie?
"Drop dead!"

What can't you say to the Loch Ness Monster?
"Go jump in the lake."

What can't you tell King Kong?
"Don't climb skyscrapers!"

Why shouldn't you get into an argument with a shark?
You'd get chewed out.

When are you most likely to dream about monsters?
When you're asleep.

What monster likes to sleep with the windows wide open?
A fresh air fiend.

Where does the Abominable Snowman sleep?
Under sheets of ice and blankets of snow.

Where do sea monsters sleep?
In water beds.

What has four "I's" and sleeps in a water bed?
The Mississippi.

Why did the ghost pull the sheets over his head?
He was practicing to be an undercover agent.

How can you tell if a monster is in bed with you?
There is an "M" on his pajamas.

What should you do if you find a monster in your bed?

Sleep somewhere else.

What prehistoric animal made noises when it slept?

A dino-snore.

Which room does a zombie sleep in?
The dead-room.

Why can vampires go days without sleep and not feel tired?

Because they sleep nights.

Why do dragons sleep during the day?

So they can fight knights (nights).

What do you call a skeleton that sleeps all day?

Lazybones.

Why did Count Dracula sleepwalk in his underwear?

He didn't have a bat-robe.

Why should you avoid vampires at dawn?

Because they like a quick bite before they go to bed.

SPOOKY SICK JOKES

"Mom, is it true that I'm a vampire?"
"Don't worry about it, son, just drink your soup before it clots."

"Mom, am I a vampire?"
"Shut up, kid, and get back in the coffin."

"Mom, what's a werewolf?"
"Never mind, dear, just comb your face."

5. GULP!

What kind of coffee does Count Dracula drink when he gets up?
  De-coffin-ated (decaffeinated).

What did the monster musician eat for breakfast?
  Rock and roll.

What do ghouls eat for breakfast?
  Shrouded Wheat.

What do ghosts eat for breakfast?
  Ghost Toasties.

What does a zombie eat for breakfast?
  Scream of Wheat.

What do witches eat for breakfast?
  Scrambled hex (eggs).

How do witches like their eggs?
  Terri-fried.

How does an egg feel when it sees a witch?
  Egg-cited.

What happens when a banana sees a witch?
  The banana splits.

What happens when a sailboat sees a witch?
  It keels over.

How do witches drink their tea?
  Out of cups and sorcerers.

What do witches order in Chinese restaurants?
  Mis-fortune cookies.

Did you hear about the monster that ate China? One hour later he was hungry again.

Why did the monster go on a diet?
To keep her ghoulish figure.

What weighs 2,000 pounds but is all bone?
A skele-ton.

STAN: How do you make a skeleton fat?
DAN: Throw him up in the air and he'll come down "plump."

What is a ghost's favorite dessert?
Ice scream (I scream).

What are Count Dracula's favorite flavors of ice cream?
Vein-illa and toothy-fruity.

What are a shark's favorite flavors of ice cream?
Sharkolate, finilla and jawberry.

How do you make a strawberry shake?
Take it to a horror movie.

What is 100-feet tall and eats tin cans?
Goatzilla.

What did Godzilla do when he was very thirsty?
He drank Canada dry.

What two things can't Godzilla have for breakfast?
Lunch and dinner.

Why does Godzilla eat raw meat?
He doesn't know how to cook.

BORIS: Why does that pig have a wooden leg?
IGOR: That pig saved my life once.
BORIS: What did he do?
IGOR: When my house caught fire, he rang the fire department. He woke me up and carried me outside to safety.
BORIS: But why does he have a wooden leg?
IGOR: Well, when you have a pig who's that wonderful, you don't eat it all at once.

What does the Abominable Snowman have for lunch?
Cold cuts.

What do sea monsters have for lunch?
Fish and ships.

A monster walked into a store and ordered an ice cream cone. When he finished eating it, he handed the clerk a ten-dollar bill. The clerk didn't think the monster knew anything about money, so he gave him back only one dollar in change.

"I hope you enjoyed the ice cream," he said to the monster. "We don't get too many monsters coming in here."

"At nine dollars an ice cream cone," said the monster, "it's no wonder."

What do little ghosts buy with their money?
Boo-ble gum.

What is big and mean and eats only candy rocks?
The Big Rock Candy Monster.

SARAH: Did you hear about the new chocolate
bar called "Shark"?
CLARA: No, what does it cost?
SARAH: Oh, an arm and a leg.

What beans do sharks like?
Human beans (beings).

What does a shark eat with peanut butter?
Jellyfish.

What is the difference between a zombie and peanut butter?

The zombie doesn't stick to the roof of your mouth.

What would you get if you crossed a jar of peanut butter and a werewolf?

A peanut butter sandwich that howls and gets hairy when the full moon comes out.

LITTLE MONSTER: Mother, I hate my teacher.
MOTHER MONSTER: Then just eat your salad, dear.

Why did the giant eat two ducks and a cow?

He wanted quackers and milk.

KING KONG: (*after catching an airplane in flight*): How do you eat one of these things?
GODZILLA: Like a peanut. You break it open and eat what's inside.

Why did Godzilla eat the bakery?

He kneaded (needed) the dough.

Why did Godzilla smash the bakery?

Because the bread was fresh.

What happened after Godzilla
swallowed the match factory?
He got heartburn.

What happened after Godzilla swallowed
the glue factory?
He got stuck up.

What happened after Godzilla swallowed
the soap factory?
He foamed at the mouth.

What happened after Godzilla swallowed
the candle factory?
He burped with delight (the light).

What happened after Godzilla swallowed
the clock factory?
He got lots of ticks.

What happened after Godzilla ate the
greenhouse?
He got window panes (pains).

HARD TO SWALLOW

What happened after Godzilla swallowed the atom bomb?

He got atomic ache.

What happened after Godzilla swallowed a dress?

He got a frock (frog) in his throat.

What happened when Godzilla swallowed the spoon?

He couldn't stir.

What happened after Godzilla swallowed his knife and fork?

He had to eat with his hands.

What happened after Godzilla ate the chicken farm?

He was in a fowl (foul) mood all day.

What happened after Godzilla ate the duck farm?

He quacked up.

How many towns can Godzilla eat on an empty stomach?

One, because after that his stomach isn't empty anymore.

JILL: I wonder what Godzilla eats?

BILL: Anything he can find.

JILL: But what if he can't find anything?

BILL: Then he eats something else.

Sign in front of shop owned by the Invisible Man:

> ## DISAPPEARED FOR LUNCH

SAL: Let's have some dessert and watch a horror movie on TV.

HAL: No, I don't want to eat peaches and scream.

What is red and white on the outside and green and lumpy on the inside?

A can of Cream of Monster soup.

How can you tell the difference between King Kong and a can of Cream of Monster soup?

Read the label.

What is a vampire's favorite soup?
Alpha-bat soup.

What is yellow, smooth and very dangerous?
Shark-infested mustard.

What is a ghoul's favorite soup?
Scream of Tomb-ato.

How do you make a mummy float?
First take two scoops of ice cream, add root beer, then drop in a mummy.

How do you make Count Dracula stew?
Keep him waiting two hours.

How can you tell if a vampire has been in your tomato juice?

By the two tiny tooth marks on the can.

What won't Count Dracula ever have for dinner?

A steak (stake). It gives him heartburn.

What do ghouls put on their potatoes?

Grave-y.

What do ghosts have with meatballs?

Spook-ghetti.

How can you tell a mummy from spaghetti?

The mummy doesn't slip off the end of your fork.

FIRST MUMMY: Can you come for dinner tonight?
SECOND MUMMY: Sorry, I'm all tied up.

Why don't mummies like natural foods?

They need all the preservatives they can get.

What happens to a pizza when it is 2,000 years old?

It gets cold.

6. FUN IN THE SUN

What is a ghost's favorite summer drink?
Ice ghoul lemonade.

Where do extinct animals go for fun and sun?
To the dino-shore.

Where do mummies go for fun and sun?
Club Dead.

What do mummies do at Club Dead?
They unwind.

Where do mummies swim?
In the Dead Sea.

What happens when mummies swim in the Dead Sea?
They get wet.

What kind of mummies live at the North Pole?
Cold ones.

GHOUL #1: My sister and I had a good time at the beach last summer. First she would bury me in the sand—then I would bury her.

GHOUL #2: Sounds like fun.

GHOUL #1: Yes—and this summer I'm going back and dig her up.

Why is a skeleton like a lost sea treasure?
It has a sunken chest.

Why did the skeleton go to the beach?
To get a skele-tan.

Why did Dr. Jekyll go to the beach?
To tan his Hyde.

Where does Dr. Jekyll relax?
In his Hyde-a-way.

Where do ghosts go sailing?
On Lake Erie (eerie).

What kind of crew sails a haunted ship?
A skeleton crew.

Did you hear about the
vampire who went to sea?
He signed up on
a blood vessel.

Count Dracula took an ocean cruise. He went into the dining room and said, "I'm starving."

"Would you like to see the menu?" asked the waiter.

"No," said Count Dracula. "Just show me the passenger list."

A boy named August was always picking fights. One day he made a mistake and picked a fight with the Frankenstein monster. The next day was the first day of September. Why?

Because it was the end of August.

What day do zombies celebrate?
April Ghoul's Day.

What does King Kong eat to celebrate the Fourth of July?
Star spangled bananas.

What do witches eat to celebrate Halloween?
Hollow-wienies.

What do werewolves eat to celebrate Halloween?
Howl-o-wienies.

What do vampires celebrate in November?
Fangsgiving.

LET'S CELEBRATE!

How do zombies celebrate New Year's Eve?

They paint the town dead.

Why don't werewolves celebrate Christmas at the beach?

They don't believe in sandy claws (Santa Claus).

Do mummies ever get presents?

Yes, on Mummy's Day.

What is a mummy after it is 2,000 years old?

2,001 years old.

What do you do with a 2,001-year-old mummy?

Wish it a happy birthday.

Why do people like to hear spooky stories in hot weather?

Because they are so chilling.

What game do little ghosts play?

Peek-a-BOO!

What game do little ghosts play with chickens?

Peck-a-BOO!

What is a little ghost's favorite game?

Haunt-and-shriek.

If you were walking along a dark street and met a Frankenstein monster, a ghost and a werewolf, what should you do?

Hope it's Halloween.

FIRST MONSTER: We had our grandfather for Christmas last year.

SECOND MONSTER: We had turkey.

7. NO-NO—KNOCK-KNOCK

Knock-knock.
  Who's there?
A-one.
  A-one who?
A-one to drink
your blood!

Knock-knock.
  Who's there?
Annie.
  Annie who?
Annie-body alive
in there?

Knock-knock.
  Who's there?
Arnold.
  Arnold who?
Arnold friend from Transylvania.

Knock-knock.
  Who's there?
Creature.
  Creature who?
Creature old friend from Transylvania with a hug!

Knock-knock.
  Who's there?
Bat.
  Bat who?
Bat you can't guess!

Knock-knock.
  Who's there?
BOO!
  Boo who?
Well, you don't have
to cry about it!

Knock-knock.
  Who's there?
Deluxe.
  Deluxe who?
Deluxe Ness Monster.

Knock-knock.
  Who's there?
Bea.
  Bea who?
Bea-ware! Tonight is
the full moon!

Knock-knock.
  Who's there?
Hair.
  Hair who?
Hair I come—
ready or not!

Knock-knock.
  Who's there?
King Kong.
  King Kong who?
King Kong, the
witch is dead . . .

Knock-knock.
  Who's there?
King Tut.
  King Tut who?
King Tut-key
Fried Chicken.

Knock-knock.
  Who's there?
Manuel.
  Manuel who?
Manuel be sorry if you
don't open this door!

Knock-knock.
  Who's there?
Piranha.
  Piranha who?
"Piranha old gray
bonnet . . ."

Knock-knock.
  Who's there?
Sinatra.
  Sinatra who?
Sinatra the cough that carries you off, it's the
coffin they carry you off in.

Knock-knock.
  Who's there?
Theresa.
  Theresa who?
Theresa full moon tonight. Look out!

Knock-knock.
  Who's there?
Voodoo.
  Voodoo who?
Voodoo you think you
are—the Wolfman?

Knock-knock.
  Who's there?
Weirdo.
  Weirdo who?
"Weirdo deer and the antelope play . . ."

Knock-knock.
  Who's there?
Yeti.
  Yeti who?
Yeti-nother knock-knock joke!

8. WILD AND WEIRD

What happened when the lamb turned into a werewolf?
It was baaa-d!

What is the difference between a werewolf and a toothpick?
If you're not sure, you'd better not pick your teeth.

How does a monster count to 18?
On its fingers.

What is a monster's normal eyesight?
20-20-20-20-20.

What do you do with a blue monster?
Cheer him up.

What do you do with a green monster?
Wait until he ripens.

If three monsters are a crowd, what are four and five?

Nine.

What does Count Dracula do at ten o'clock?
He takes a coffin break.

Why do dragons have long tales?
They can't remember short stories.

PIT: What's the difference between a dragon and a matterbaby?
PAT: What's a matterbaby?
PIT: Nothing, sweetie. What's the matter with you?

Why did the knight buy a can of insecticide?
To kill the dragonfly.

What would you get if you crossed a green monster and a pen?
The Ink-redible Hulk.

What would you get if you crossed King Kong, Superman and a bug?
A 600-pound cockroach that could leap the Empire State Building at a single bound.

What would you get if you crossed the Frankenstein monster and the Invisible Man?
I don't know what you'd call it, but it wouldn't be much to look at.

What is the difference between zombies and darned socks?
Zombies are dead men; darned socks are men-ded.

RICK: What's the difference between a zombie and a potfor?
DICK: What's a potfor?
RICK: To cook in, dummy!

What law do all ghouls obey?
The Law of Grave-ity (gravity).

COUNT DRACULA'S
FAVORITE THINGS

What is his favorite animal?
A giraffe.

What is his favorite city?
Vein-ice (Venice).

What is his favorite picnic spot?
The bat-anical gardens.

Who is his favorite chef?
Batty Crocker.

What is his favorite kind of eyes?
The bloodshot type.

What is his favorite snack?
A fangfurter.

What is his favorite fruit?
The nectarine.

What is his favorite disease?
High blood pressure.

What is a ghoul's favorite plant?
Poison ivy.

What is King Kong's favorite flower?
Chimp-pansies.

MAD SCIENTIST: What has teeth and flies through the air?
IGOR: A flying saw, sir.

What can't you give a headless body?
A headache.

Who saw the Tyrannosaurus rex sneak into the restaurant?

The diners saw (dinosaur).

What dinosaur is hard to ride?

A Bronco-saurus.

How do you get a dinosaur to do something right away?

You say, "Pronto-saurus!"

How do you make a dinosaur hurry up?

You say, "Shake a leg-o-saurus!"

Where would you go to buy a Brontosaurus?
To the dino-store.

When Count Dracula goes to the barber, does he get a haircut?
No, he gets all of them cut.

Where does Count Dracula get his hair cut?
At the ends.

What would you get if you crossed an onion and Count Dracula?
Either an onion that sucks blood or a vampire with watery eyes.

What would you get if you crossed a comedian and Count Dracula?
Someone who laughs at the sight of blood.

What would you get if you crossed a dog and Count Dracula?
I don't know, but its bite would be worse than its bark.

When is a haunted house not on land and not on water?
When it is on fire.

Why is a haunted house like a rabbit farm?
They're both hair-(hare)raising.

THAT GIANT IS SO BIG—

HOW BIG IS HE?

That giant is so big, he has to stand on a ladder just to shave himself.

That giant is so big, he has to get on his knees to put his hands in his pockets.

That giant is so big—that when it rains, he lies down and uses his feet as an umbrella. Then when the sun comes out, he does the same thing to get some shade.

What is a ghost's favorite thing on a farm?
The scarecrow.

What did the monster say to the scarecrow?
"I can beat the stuffing out of you."

What did the pecan tree say to the monster who was shaking it?
"Stop pecan (picking) on me!"

What did the maple tree say to the monster?
"Leaf me alone!"

What did the Frankenstein monster say when he ran out of electricity?
"A.C. come, A.C. go."

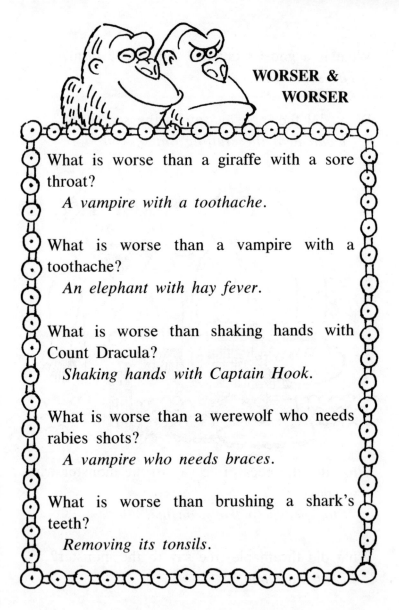

WORSER & WORSER

What is worse than a giraffe with a sore throat?

A vampire with a toothache.

What is worse than a vampire with a toothache?

An elephant with hay fever.

What is worse than shaking hands with Count Dracula?

Shaking hands with Captain Hook.

What is worse than a werewolf who needs rabies shots?

A vampire who needs braces.

What is worse than brushing a shark's teeth?

Removing its tonsils.

LITTLE MONSTER: Mama, may I eat New York?

MOTHER MONSTER: Only if you wash your hands first.

How do you tell Godzilla from a bunny rabbit?
You don't tell Godzilla anything!

How do you tell an elephant from a skeleton?
Wait for the wind to blow. The one with the flapping ears is the elephant.

What kind of ant is fifteen feet tall?
A gi-ant.

What is big and blue?
A giant holding its breath.

What is the only bird that can lift a giant?
A crane.

Can a giant have a nose twelve inches long?
No. If its nose were twelve inches long, it would be a foot.

Two lazy hillbillies were lying under a tree near a swamp. One of them spotted a huge alligator.

"Mind it there, Clem, there's a big alligator about to snap off your foot."

Clem slowly looked up and said, "Hey there, Lem, which foot?"

How long should a monster's legs be?
Long enough to reach the ground.

Which side of the werewolf has the most fur?
The outside.

What kind of fur do you get from a werewolf?
As fur as you can get.

Why do werewolves have fur coats?
Because they'd look silly in plastic ones.

Why did the vampire wear a black belt?
To keep his pants up.

Why did the vampire wear yellow suspenders?
To keep his shoulders down.

What do little ghouls wear in the rain?
Ghoul-oshes (goulashes).

Which giant wore the biggest shoes?
The one with the biggest feet.

Why was the giant wearing Reeboks?
Because his Adidas were in the wash.

9. SCHOOL SPIRIT

DON: I didn't know our school was haunted!

RON: Neither did I. How did you find out?

DON: Everybody's been talking about our school spirit!

Where do little zombies go on weekdays?
To ghoul school.

Who teaches ghoul school?
A creature teacher.

What was the first thing King Kong learned in school?
The Ape-B-C's.

What is the first thing that little ghosts learn in school?
Not to spook until they're spooken to.

How do little ghosts learn to count?
One, boo, three, four, five, six, seven, hate, nine, fright-ten!

What is the first thing little serpents learn in school?
Hiss-tory.

What is the first thing little vampires learn?
The alpha-bat.

Why do little vampires stay up all night?
They have to study for blood tests.

What kind of tests do little witches have to study for?
Hex-aminations.

What is the first thing little witches learn in school?
Spelling.

Where do little knights learn to kill dragons?
In night (knight) school.

How do little skeletons study for tests?
They bone up the night before.

MAN-EATING MONSTER #1: Tommy was sent home from school today.
MAN-EATING MONSTER #2: What did he do?
MAN-EATING MONSTER #1: They caught him buttering up the teacher.

HOW DO YOU GET RID OF A MONSTER?

I DON'T KNOW. HOW DO YOU GET RID OF A MONSTER?

Give him an airplane ticket and tell him to take off.

Give him a tissue and tell him to blow.

Give him a pogo stick and tell him to hop it.

Give him a jump rope and tell him to skip out.

Why did the one-eyed monster close down his school?

Because he had only one pupil.

What's green and shiny and teaches 5th grade?
The teacher from the Black Lagoon.

What would happen if you crossed a vampire and a teacher?
You'd get more blood tests than ever.

Where do zombies go after junior high?
To highs ghoul.

TEACHER: Arthur, where are you?
ARTHUR: Here in the closet.
TEACHER: What are you doing there?
ARTHUR: Didn't you tell me to read *Dr. Jekyll and Hyde*?

FAMOUS GHOULS

What ghoul discovered the New World in 1492?
Christopher Ghoul-umbus.

What ghoul was a president?
Ghoul-ysses S. Grant.

Who was the most famous ghoul in French history?
Charles de Ghoul (de Gaulle).

SPOOKY BIOGRAPHIES

1. *Jack the Ripper* by I. Cut M. Upp
2. *King Kong* by Harry Ape
3. *My Life as a Monster* by I. Ben Badd
4. *The Invisible Person* by Les Noticeable
5. *Mummies of Old* by Anne Teak

What do you find in haunted libraries?
BOO-ks!

How does a book about zombies begin?
With a dead-ication (dedication).

What story do little zombies like to hear at bedtime?
"Ghoul-dilocks and the Three Bears."

What comic book do vampires like to read at bedtime?
Batman.

Who is the most famous shark writer?
William Sharkspeare.

What famous book do ghouls read in school?
Ghouliver's (Gulliver's) Travels.

SPOOKY BESTSELLERS

1. *Swamp Romances* by Ali Gator and Crockett Dial
2. *Bitten by a Vampire* by Lord Howard Hertz
3. *Poisonous Snakes* by Sir Pent
4. *Hunting Fossils* by Dinah Saur
5. *First Class Burials* by M. T. Cass Kett
6. *Living with the Frankenstein Monster* by I. M. Nutts
7. *Tombstone Inscriptions* by Eppie Taff
8. *Successful Hangings* by Art E. Chokes
9. *Great Monsters of the World in Color* by Claus N. Fangs
10. *Visiting Haunted Houses* by Hugo Furst

What kind of books do zombies read?
Books with a cemetery plot.

What does a hangman read every day?
The noosepaper.

What newspapers do dinosaurs read?
The Prehistoric Times.

What has two heads, four lips and should keep its mouth shut?

A monster chewing bubble gum.

What has six legs, four arms and goes "Crunch, crunch"?

A monster eating potato chips.

Who sewed flags all day and flapped wings at night?

Bat-sy Ross.

FIRST MONSTER: That girl over there rolled her eyes at me. What should I do?

SECOND MONSTER: A real gentlemen would pick them up and roll them back to her.

LEARNING HOW TO TALK TO MONSTERS

What should you say when you meet Count Dracula?
   "Hello, sucker!"

What should you say when you meet a two-headed monster?
   "Hello, hello!"

What is the polite thing to say when you meet a werewolf?
   "How-lo, there!"

How should undertakers speak to each other?
   Gravely.

What should you call a monster with no ears?
   Anything you want—he can't hear you.

How should you talk to a giant?
   Use BIG words.

LEARNING HOW TO TALK TO MONSTERS

What should you call a giant with a bad temper?
"Sir."

What should you call an eight-foot-tall giant?
"Shortie."

How should you talk to Godzilla?
Politely.

What is the best way to talk to the Frankenstein monster?
By long distance.

How should rattlesnakes talk to each other on the phone?
Poison-to-poison.

Why doesn't it pay to talk to a monster with four lips?
All you get is double talk.

MONSTER ROYALTY QUIZ

What Egyptian queen was a vampire?
Cleo-bat-ra.

Who was the biggest monarch in history?
King Kong.

What ghost haunted a King of England?
The Spirit of '76.

Why don't many ghosts go to college?
Because so few graduate from high school.

What do you say when King Kong graduates?
"Kong-gratulations!"

What do you say when Count Dracula graduates?
"Con-dracula-tions!"

10. DON'T YOU DARE!

What do you call a monster who devours everything in its path?

Lonesome.

When did Dr. Frankenstein stop being lonely?

When he learned how to make new friends.

Why did the Frankenstein monster go out with a prune?

Because he couldn't get a date.

Who do sea monsters date?

They go out with the tide.

Who do ghouls date?

Anyone they can dig up.

Where do ghosts pick up their mail?

At the ghost office.

How does a letter from a ghost begin?

"Tomb (to whom) it may concern . . ."

What happened when the werewolf met the starlet?

It was love at first bite.

What happened when the two boa constrictors met?

They got a crush on each other.

What did the boy monster say to the girl monster?

"I want to hold your hand, hand, hand, hand . . ."

What did the boy rattlesnake say to the girl rattlesnake?

"Give me a little hiss."

How do vampires kiss?
Very carefully.

FIRST GIRL MONSTER: What is your new boyfriend like?

SECOND GIRL MONSTER: He's mean, low, nasty, dirty, ugly—and those are just his good points.

FIRST GHOST: My girlfriend is a medium.

SECOND GHOST: Is that so? Mine is a large.

MANNY: If Godzilla were here, would you like to see me put my head in his mouth?

FANNY: Sure.

MANNY: And I thought you were a friend of mine!

How do you send a ghost a letter?
By scare (air) mail.

How do you get in touch with the Loch Ness Monster?
Drop him a line.

THAT MONSTER IS
SO REPULSIVE—

HOW
REPULSIVE
IS HE?

He's so repulsive that when he throws a boomerang it doesn't come back.

He's so repulsive that when he plays hide-and-seek nobody looks for him.

He's so repulsive that when he goes to the zoo, the monkeys throw peanuts at him.

JOE MONSTER: Do you mind holding my hand?
JEAN MONSTER: Not at all.
JOE MONSTER: Here it is. I'll be back for it in an
  hour.

FIRST MONSTER: Sorry, I must have lost my
head.
SECOND MONSTER: Well, don't worry about it—
you still have the other one.

PATIENT: Can a person be in love with Godzilla?
DOCTOR: Definitely not! Next question.
PATIENT: Do you know anyone who wants to buy
a very large engagement ring?

Did you hear about the monsters
who got married? They loved
each shudder (other).

Did you hear about the vampires
who couldn't get married? They
loved in vein.

SILLY: Did Count Dracula ever get married?
WILLY: No, he was a bat-chelor (bachelor).

What did the girl Frankenstein monster say to the
boy Frankenstein monster?
"You're so electrocute."

Why did the boy monster whistle at the girl
monster?
Because she had nice legs, legs, legs, legs . . .

DID YOU HEAR
THE JOKE ABOUT:

the shark: it's a real killer!

the witch's broom: it's sweeping the nation!

the werewolf: it's a howl!

the killer bees: it's a honey!

the prison breakout: it's a riot!

the owl: it's a hoot!

the scary movie: it's a scream!

the germ: it's sickening!

the dynamite: it's a blast!

the toothless vampire: it's pointless!

How does a graveyard love story begin?
Boy meets ghoul.

Why do demons and ghouls get along so well?
Because demons are a ghoul's best friend.

It is a lovely summer evening. Johnny and Jane are parked on a hill overlooking town. Johnny turns to Jane and says, "Jane, sweetheart, I have some good news and some bad news. The good news is that any moment we will see a beautiful full moon rise over the hill."

"Oh, you're so romantic," Jane says. "But what is the bad news?"

"I'm a werewolf and the full moon drives me mad. Aaaaagh!"

There was a young phantom named Paul
Who went to a fancy dress ball.
  To shock every guest
  He went there undressed,
But no one could see him at all.

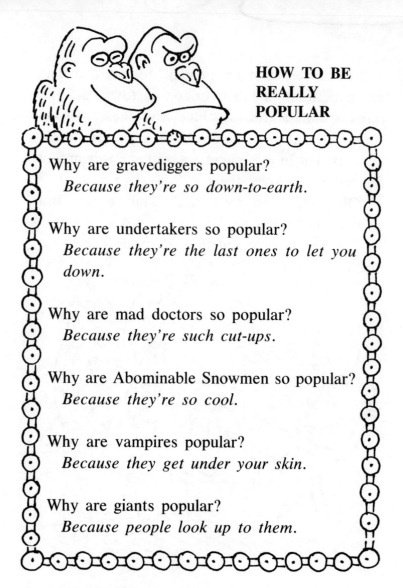

HOW TO BE REALLY POPULAR

Why are gravediggers popular?
Because they're so down-to-earth.

Why are undertakers so popular?
Because they're the last ones to let you down.

Why are mad doctors so popular?
Because they're such cut-ups.

Why are Abominable Snowmen so popular?
Because they're so cool.

Why are vampires popular?
Because they get under your skin.

Why are giants popular?
Because people look up to them.

Where do fortune-tellers dance?
At the crystal ball.

Where do Abominable Snowmen dance?
At the snowball.

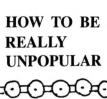

HOW TO BE REALLY UNPOPULAR

Why don't people like vampires?
Because they're a pain in the neck.

Why don't people like executioners?
Because they're always hanging around.

Why don't people like Abominable Snowmen?
Because it's too hard to warm up to them.

Why don't people like mummies?
Because they're all wrapped up in themselves.

Why don't people like skeletons?
Because they've got no heart.

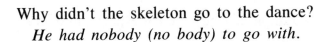

Why didn't the skeleton go to the dance?
He had nobody (no body) to go with.

What music do mummies dance to?
Ragtime.

What song do monsters sing about their girlfriends?
"The Ghoul That I Marry . . ."

What does a ghost bride throw to her bridesmaids?
A boo-quet (bouquet).

TRENT: Did you hear about the monster debutante that had a coming-out party?
BRENT: No, what happened?
TRENT: They made her go back in.

Why is Godzilla a big hit at parties?
Because he is tons of fun.

Why are werewolves a big hit at parties?
Because they're a howl.

Why don't zombies get more invitations?
Because they're never the life of the party.

What do werewolves sing at parties?
"Howl, howl, the gang's all hair . . ."

What do vampires sing when the party is over?
"Auld Fang Syne."

11. THIS IS THE END!

What four letters do you ask a friend who just met Dracula?

R-U-O-K.

What four letters would really surprise the Invisible Man?

O-I-C-U.

When the executioner registered at the hotel, the clerk asked him what kind of room he wanted. "Oh," said the executioner, "my needs are small. I just want a place to hang my hat and a few friends."

What is the first thing a witch rings for in a hotel?

B-room service.

Why do witches fly brooms?

Because vacuum cleaners don't have long enough cords.

What is the most important safety rule for witches?

Don't fly off the handle.

GWEN: Why are you snapping your fingers?
BEN: To keep the ghosts away.
GWEN: But there are no ghosts around here.
BEN: You see? It works!

Why was the ghost on the magazine cover?
Because she was BOO-tiful.

Did you hear about the monster who went to the beauty parlor?

They wouldn't let her in.

GREG MONSTER: Are the monsters in your town ugly?
MEG MONSTER: Are they ugly! We held a beauty contest last year and nobody won.

What song do monsters play at beauty pageants?
"A pretty ghoul is like a malady . . ."

TOM: Did you hear about the woman who smeared vanishing cream all over herself?
DICK: No, what happened?
TOM: No one knows.

Where does a witch keep her wallet?
In a hag bag.

Why is a bad witch like a candle?
Both are wick-ed.

What do you get if you cross a cobra and a witch?
A snake charmer.

What do you get if you cross a witch and a mummy?
A flying Band-Aid.

What do you hear if you cross a witch's broom and a clock?

The broom's tick (broomstick).

What is yellow, shoots webs and jumps from building to building?

Spider Banana.

What wears a black cape, flies through the air and bites people?

A mosquito in a black cape.

What is green and wrinkled and goes through walls?

Casper, the Friendly Pickle.

AL: What is the difference between a lemon, a monster and a bag of cement?

VAL: I don't know. What?

AL: You can squeeze a lemon, but you can't squeeze a monster.

VAL: What about the bag of cement?

AL: I threw that in to make it hard.

TED: What's the difference between vampires and snoo?

FRED: What's snoo?

TED: Nothing much, really. What's snoo with you?

What is the difference between Count Dracula and a grape?

The grape is purple.

What does Dracula visit when he goes to New York?

The Vampire State Building.

Why did King Kong climb the Empire State Building?

To catch a plane.

If Dracula and King Kong jumped off the top of the Empire State Building, who would land first?

Who cares!

GERTIE MONSTER: If I had a face like yours, I'd put it on a wall and throw a brick at it.

BERTIE MONSTER: If I had a face like yours, I'd put it on a brick and throw a wall at it.

Sam, a waiter who had worked in the same restaurant for years, passed away. His wife missed him terribly. One day she went to the restaurant, sat down at a table and called to him.

"Sam, Sam, where are you?" she sobbed.

Miraculously—and very softly—a voice replied, "Here I am."

"Sam!" she gasped, "Sam, is that you? Speak louder, I can barely hear you!"

"I can't speak louder," came the almost inaudible voice.

"Well, then," begged his wife, "Can you come a little closer?"

"Impossible," Sam whispered. "That's not my table."

Who gives a speech after a ghost banquet?
The after-dinner spooker.

Sign in fortune-teller's window:

MEDIUM PRICES

HOW DO YOU GET RID OF A MONSTER?

I DON'T KNOW. HOW DO YOU GET RID OF A MONSTER?

Give him a drum and tell him to beat it.

Give him an egg and tell him to splatter.

Give him an eraser and tell him to disappear.

Give him a pair of scissors and tell him to cut out.

Give him a beehive and tell him to buzz off.

Give him a map and tell him to get lost.

Give him a ball and tell him to roll away.

What do you say when you hear a noise in the cemetery?
  "Halt, who ghost there?"

What goes around a cemetery but doesn't move?
  A fence.

Sign in front of the cemetery:

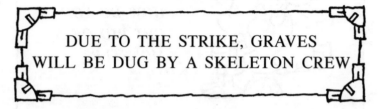

DUE TO THE STRIKE, GRAVES
WILL BE DUG BY A SKELETON CREW

How wide is a cemetery?
  A grave yard.

Why was the cemetery crowded?
  Everyone was dying to get in.

FLIP: Did you hear about the price rise at the cemetery?
FLOP: Yes, and they're blaming it on the cost of living.

How far can you walk into a cemetery?
  Only halfway. After that you're walking out.

Who is the main ghost in Congress?
  The Spooker (Speaker) of the House.

What business is King Kong in?
Monkey business.

Why did King Kong climb to the top of the Empire State Building?
Because he couldn't fit into the elevator.

How do you catch King Kong's attention?
Climb a tree and make a noise like a banana.

What do you get if you cross King Kong and a Boy Scout?
A monkey that's always prepared.

What do you get if you cross a ghoul and a Boy Scout?
A ghoul that helps old ladies cross the street.

NELL: Do ghouls act peculiar?

DELL: No, they just do what comes supernaturally.

GARY: How much will you charge to haunt my boss?

GHOST: For $10 I promise to scare him out of his wits.

GARY: Well, here's $5. He's only a half-wit.

What do you call a vampire that faints at the sight of blood?

A failure.

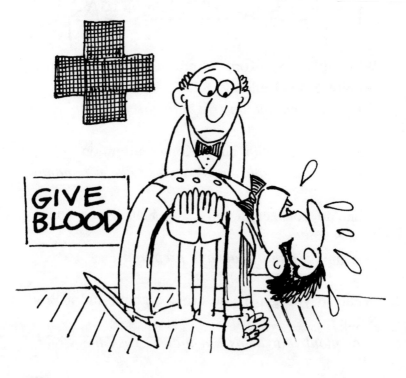

Why wouldn't Count Dracula settle down?
Because he was a fly-by-night.

Why was Count Dracula hanging around the computers?
He was trying to get a byte.

What happened when the dragon breathed on the computers?
He got baked Apples.

What do you get if you cross a giant and a computer?
A ten-ton know-it-all.

What do vampires learn in business school?
How to type blood.

Why did the monster secretary cut her fingers off?
She wanted to write shorthand.

Who buries Honda bikes?
A Honda-taker.

Sign in funeral parlor:

SATISFACTION GUARANTEED
OR YOUR MUMMY BACK

MUSEUM GUIDE: The mummy in that case is 2,006 years old.

VISITOR: Amazing! How do you know it's exactly 2,006 years old?

MUSEUM GUIDE: Well, it was 2,000 years old when I started working here, and I've been here for six years.

DICK: My father collects things. He has a 3,000-year-old mummy.

JANE: That's nothing. My father has an Adam's apple.

Why was King Tut buried in a pyramid?
Because he was dead.

What do you hear when King Tut falls into the Black Sea?
"Splash!"

TIMMY: Daddy, when were you in Egypt?
FATHER: I never was in Egypt.
TIMMY: Then where did you get my Mummy?

FIRST MUMMY: That fellow just sold me the Nile River.
SECOND MUMMY: Egypt you!

Where did they bury the crossword puzzle fan?
Six feet down and three across.

What time is it when Count Dracula leaves his coffin?
Time to run.

How many sides does a coffin have?
Two. The inside and the outside.

OSCAR: When I die, I want to be cremated.
FELIX: That would be just like you—to go away and leave ashes all over the house.

Why can't a man living in New York be buried in California?

Because he is still alive.

When do monsters remind you of creatures from outer space?

When they're Martian along.

What would you get if you crossed a mummy and a bell?

A dead ringer.

What bell climbed the Empire State Building?

King Gong.

What would you get if you crossed a pigeon, a frog and a Tyrannosaurus rex?

A pigeon-toed (toad) dinosaur.

What would you get if you crossed a dragon, an onion and an owl?

A dragon that has bad breath, but doesn't give a hoot.

What would you get if you crossed a vampire and a ghoul?

I don't know. But I don't think I want to hang around long enough to find out.

If a werewolf lost its tail, where could it buy a new one?

In a retail store.

NIT: Is it true that a werewolf won't attack you if you carry a good luck charm?

WIT: That depends on how fast you carry it.

GUS: How do you lead a werewolf?

RUSS: Simple. First you get a rope. Then you tie the rope to the werewolf—

GUS: And then?

RUSS: Then you find out where the werewolf wants to go.

A hillbilly loved his rifle. When it broke and couldn't be fixed, he buried it. What did he put on the tombstone?

GUN
BUT NOT
FORGOTTEN

GOODBYE

How do you say good-bye to a mummy?
"B.C'ing you!"

How do you say good-bye to King Kong?
"Ape be seeing you!"

How do you say good-bye to the Abominable Snowman?
"Have an ice day!"

INDEX